Praise for Carrie Magness Radna:

"What is excellent and fine in this world is not often come by easy, nor held so easily fast. In *Hurricanes Never Apologize,* Carrie Magness Radna provides the reader with extraordinary testimony in support of that contention. The speaker in many of these poems is battle-worn, but never defeated — wresting soft and flowing cadences from the heavy keys of a piano, confronting the dark matter disguised as ancient stars in our psyche, catching her breath in the bittersweet embrace of an eternal seeker who has reached the end of her days with her soul still searching.

There is a steeliness to these poems, even at their most vulnerable, that rewards. Even in the most bleak or challenging of moments, when she reminds us that even in the inevitable moments of darkness, 'the light will eventually come again', Ms. Radna offers us this: *Words are the only currency I can afford/Music the only God I pray to.* That's a mantra of solace and resolve we all might pay heed to.

Dive into this book and experience great ventures of the cosmos and the human heart — quarried in equal measure from the momentous and the small, revealed in chance glimpses of the sacred, savored in the rare moments of reflective calm *with any roof overhead*. At their best, these poems are pure vision, assembled, dispersed, reassembled from the eternal existential dust."

-George Wallace,
Writer in residence, Walt Whitman Birthplace

"Carrie Magness Radna wears her words as a protest on her poetic sleeve. Her stories mesmerize, address present day anger. America is under siege, and the world is in crisis mode. Wars never cease, the seas are rising, the polar caps are melting, et al. Our planet is in danger of self-destructing. In *Hurricanes Never Apologize,* Ms. Radna asks us not to apologize, but to cherish whom we love and motivate ourselves to save the world and ourselves from extinction."

> -Patricia Carragon, Curator, Editor-in-Chief of
> Brownstone Poets, Brooklyn, NY,
> author of *Meowku* and *The Cupcake Chronicles.*

"Carrie Magness Radna is an accomplished, richly talented poet and vocalist whose poetry personifies nature, brings the cosmic down to earth, and demonstrates how our disintegrations oddly fits a divine purpose, She dwells on how love fits within our daily pathos—and because Eastern mystical philosophy warns against desire, she notes how the word pathos has a root that means passion, so that, within her work we see admonishments against desiring too fervently. Yet, her words are painfully redolent with writhing humanity, chaotic in gut-clenched pain. Feminist pride glows through in "Women's Names Sensual Series" poems laced throughout her book. This poet will yearn for the sleep that *knits the raveled sleeve of care;* but she is no slacker, stays wide awake, and launches fervent jeremiads against the Anti-Everything that infests our White House. Reading her is a flammable experience."

> -Arthur Gatti, author of *Songs of Mute Eagles*
> and winner of The Dwight Durling Award
> (CUNY-wide writing contest)

Hurricanes Never Apologize

Poems by Carrie Magness Radna

Luchador Press
Big Tuna, TX

Copyright © Carrie Magness Radna, 2019
First Edition1 3 5 7 9 10 8 6 4 2
ISBN: 978-1-950380-72-5
LCCN: 2019954974

Design, edits and layout: El Dopa
Cover image: Jon Lee Grafton
Title page image: Carrie Magness Radna
Author photo: Carrie Magness Radna
All rights reserved. No part of this publication may be reproduced or transmitted in any form or by any means, electronic or mechanical, including photocopying, recording or by info retrieval system, without prior written permission from the author.

The author would like to thank the editors of these publications where some of the poems in this collection originally appeared:

"Crossing the border: The Poetic Bond VIII" (*Willowbrook Press:* published December 6, 2018) and 2018 *Riverside Anthology* (March 2, 2019)

"Is This Now America" & "Independence Day" 2018: *Tuck Magazine* (July 6, 2018): http://tuckmagazine.com/2018/07/06/poetry-1595/

"Remembering 9/11:" *Tuck Magazine* (Sept. 14, 2018): http://tuckmagazine.com/2018/09/14/poetry-1723/

"Rose Season:" Remembering as I go walking (*Boxwood Star Press:* published August 23, 2019)

"Remembrance Day:" *Nomad's Choir* (Fall 2019)

"Dust:" *Nomad's Choir* (Spring 2021)

Table of Contents

Michael's Wind / 1

I Wear My Sadness Like a Shirt / 2

Dust / 4

Home, Now and After Death / 6

Resentment / 8

Rose Season / 10

Pathos / 12

Is This Now America / 14

Remembering 9/11 / 16

Sinister City / 17

Transparency / 19

Emotional Holocaust / 21

Crossing the Border / 24

Twenty Years / 25

Suspended Animation / 27

Army of Ghosts / 30

Army Oranges / 31

Remembrance Day / 34

Ursula (No. 58 Of Women's Names Sensual Series) / 36

Frigg (No. 12 Of Women's Names Sensual Series) / 38

Elegy for Hawking / 41

Mind-Thought Police / 42

Tainted (Until Now) / 44

Dark Thoughts / 45

Dark Matter (In Human Scale) / 48

River Styx Today (No. 36 Of E Verses) / 49

Dance with Death (Remembering Nana, 1925-2006) / 50

Haunted / 51

In Passing (No. 45 Of E Verses) / 53

Angels On The Shelf (No. 43 Of E Verses) / 54

White is the Color of Death / 55

To my kickass sister Devon and brother D.J.,
& my sibs gained by marriage,
Courtney, Raffi, Rebeka & Dev:

You are the lights shining in the darkest night sky.
I love you all!

Michael's Wind

Not nice to already resign that this is a clunker of a poem,
honed by dead-boned tiredness—today is a true Fall day
at 55 degrees, wind is at 30 mph; it's time for medium
    sweaters
and jackets. Hurricane Michael has decimated Florida,
wreaking its havoc in the Carolinas, but its wind is now
    traveling North.

I knew a Michael once. He was constantly moving,
    a slave of ADHD.
At least when he knocked over the breakfast table, in the
    morning
after we made love the first time (my first time), he was
immediately contrite, dripping with apologies as the milk
ran down the table's legs. Hurricanes never apologize.

Just have their fun and be done with it—that was Mike too,
when he dumped me a month afterward via email. There was
another woman waiting in the background,
making her powerful landfall—upon him.

This poem is unexpected,
like most storms and sexual conquests.

I Wear His Sadness Like a Shirt

When I heard the news
of the passing of an old friend
of my friend,
I want to keep him company
I wear his sadness like a shirt

His smiles and jokes he wears outside I see
with his chosen family,
until we are alone in empty hallways
I feel his profound loss
through his soft gaze
I wear his sadness like a shirt

No time for brewing tea,
the moving men are here
to carry the rest of the room's contents away,
the walls are white and empty,
his shirt is black and cotton
I wear his sadness like a shirt

Loss does not feel like cotton,
more like heavy wool
one's skin can't breathe in,
and we both breathed so easy
as we held each other

I wear his sadness like a shirt

I wish I could stay
for the rest of the night's song,
but his love is coming home soon,
and I wish he could feel my love
(it would make him breathe easy like cotton)

Leaving him was so hard to do,
especially since he left his loss with me

Right now, at 2 am,
I let my own emotions take center stage,
tears fell down my nose,
my heart beating hard in my chest.

I wish I didn't have to leave him;
I wear his sadness like a shirt

Dust

> Part of a possible 21st Century humanistic Requiem
> (based on the 3rd movement of Johannes Brahms's
> *Ein deutsches Requiem,* "Herr, lehre doch mich"

If God is one of the favored architects
of every hidden pocket universe,
then Science is its learned
master engineer—

Only dust
lasts forever
traveling from all points of
hidden space,
from a hairbreadth
of dying stars
we are created
even from evolution
from centuries of floating
particles from
hundreds of light years
we are all formed
from the elements of Earth

insignificant particles
we all are
ending as dust
many years from now

we all are ancient
stars drifting

Death will come for all of us
we will all become dust
hovering from Earth
freely into the
solar system

Home, Now and After Death

Part of a possible 21st Century humanistic Requiem
(based on the 4th movement of *Ein deutsches Requiem:*
"Wie lieblich sind deine Wohnungen")

1.

An essential equilibrium
one feels and finds
at home sweet home,
that all is right & just
where food is shared,
beds are made,
families are together

The bubble is filled
with promises, rules, secrets & lies
loved ones take to the grave.

What is the perfect house
where everyone under the moon
can dwell in?

without angry shouting,
without hunger,
without abandonment,
abuse or neglect?

2.

After death,
do we end up under one,
monstrous golden castle
where God is rumored
to live in?

How will we all fit in there?
Or, do we evaporate into free air
& become swirling dust?

3.

In the end,
when we leave only souvenirs
behind, our memories
are kept safe in our old houses,
our portraits
keeping watch in darkened halls

I am content
with any roof overhead
as long as you
are here with me.

Resentment

Does this fit oddly like knives piercing in your gut, only in
    odd moments
where liquor is abundant, and when the hormones cause you
    to weep
over adorable children, once again?
Or it is constantly moving upon the thinnest, tiniest
    Möbius strip
that only you can see or touch?

It will age you prematurely, pickle you in bitter brine,
make you holler and whine during those odd moments
when you look your best or worst.

The curse of comparing yourself against others, without any
    compassion
towards one's self, is exhausting, so why is the drama of it
    so intoxicating?
I have things I am proud of, but they haven't come by easy.
I can carve words from imaginary oceans, but my messages
    are only heard by a few people;
the ones that swim freely without university influence (in
    composing)
and people don't like complainers, but, in this particular
case…

Even in my destitute state, creative musings are rich in
    my mind;
they taste sweet as golden candy, as the stars feel ecstatic,
my moods grow elastic between each time I'm kissed.

Rose Season

We lingered in the rose garden
blooming fast in Great Neck
without any consequences,
except the rose-colored rash
my skin wore
early this morning.

Who knew we would wonder so far and so long?

I thought about the terrorist attack
in Orlando the night before,
a madman killing 50 individuals
in Pulse, a gay nightclub;
they all went there to relax,
have fun and feel they belonged
in a safe place.

Will it ever feel safe again out there?

During this bittersweet day,
the day after, back in Long Island
I saw many beautiful things:
dancers gliding to Chopin,
Brahms and Scriabin
(among many others),
the piano with heavy keys played by an expert

who made the cadences soft and flowing,
making new friends on the ride to the train,
and now, the roses in the garden,
representing every shape and color.

Loss should make people stronger, realizing *never again*,
every act, callous or not, has a consequence.

Even when the lights of life are extinguished,
the roses fall to the ground as petals and nothing more,
they will always be remembered
and cherished, not forgotten;
darkness is never forever,
the light will eventually come again,
new roses will bloom in the next season,
new life will take root,
wearing each one of our faces.

Pathos

At the end of the life of each ancient Greek, they only asked one question: *Did he have passion?*

Pathos, the word for passion,
is now roughly translated as sorrow.

Many wars and shifts in reasoning
may had dulled or shifted the seasoning
the first original Eros, separated from erotica, enthusiasm,
    even simmering
the odd ducks, who crave to sit
upon the great thinkers' laps,
reading their words loud to a captive audience.

But accents are often changed to get ahead, books hidden,
    family names Anglicized, works authored by those only
known by their initials; holy writings favored over romances,
    family duties lie waiting.

People love the wrong ones; passion becomes sorrow.

My love is covered in gaffa tape of pathos, shifting between one extreme to the other, caught in mid-suspension, barely breathing.

My passion, I keep it hidden
when the sorrows come creeping, finally letting it
    out of its cage
in the tender moments before sleeping.

Is This Now America

Thanks to the latest news,
my heart is flattened like a National flag,
folded over and over again,
its stars are still showing;

(don't want to touch the ground,
don't want to be burned,
I want to fly free and high,
but it's never the right time)

Children are still separated from their parents (for profits),
their families just want a taste of freedom, away from their
    insurmountable hardships.

Mr. President,
why are you making their lives harder?
When will they be reunited,
when the background checks and important forms have
    been filed?

Is this now America,
whitewashing immigrants?
Is this now America,
not owning up to our foibles and mistakes?

My heart is like a flag;
I want it to spread it out
and inspire everyone I see
oh say can you see

Thanks to those in charge,
our little lives are beginning
(not) to count,

(and with these stripes we are healed)
and we do feel the pain
while the marks remain invisible,
invincible

Remembering 9/11

All the clouds sat down
in Columbus Circle
during the morning rush.

Everyone was strangely quiet,
all the birds screamed: *Hush!*

But the 17th Day of Remembrance
for 9/11 is now over; prayers said,
loved ones comforted, songs sung.

At 50th Street, changing from C to E,
I had to continue downtown to travel
up,
it pointed towards World Trade Center,
my heart was suddenly hung
out to dry in a humid place.

People on the train were solemn, respectful, some had
    tears in their eyes—
disguised as boredom across their faces.

Wish I could wake up,
and that the world's madness would eventually
stop.

Sinister City

Tracing the blotchy words
upon the water-stained paper
of the old textbook,
the ideas printed there
are no longer revolutionary

This city, once spoiled by war
is ruined with hidden terrors;
the men in charge
want to be dictators,
all the young, brilliant girls
are banned from higher education

The prettiest girls
are groomed as decent models
of womanhood,
chosen by the great Papa leaders
as robotic, dancing street crossing guards,
some learned three languages
but only in secret.

The men, taught to be powerful
with words and fists,
they surrendered to the Army;
their hunger for money grows
as their comrades fell,
perishing on the bloody fields.

Over time,
the buildings grew taller
and were painted over;
the young saplings
were cut down in their prime.

Each May Day
is a day of rest from work.
The members of the
sinister city could breathe
and play in the fields,
barbecuing meats in a pot
and spending their
hard-earned beer coupons
issued by the government

One day
the whole city breathes
easy in the park

Transparency

Light gathers on the window;
it wants to breathe, to come in
it stings my eyes as I wake up,
this last trip really did me in

My roots are present,
but they haven't dug in deep;
they ride right under the Earth's surface,
and they stretch towards the corners of the world

Still trying to find
my own space in this world—

There's no filter available,
I take everyone's energy in,
even imagining I'm in a box on the subway,
all the people still peer in—

I've become more transparent
with each passing year,
like the light outside that tries to get in,
but he wants to stay safe in the darkness,
he never wants to walk on the beach
or take a swim;
and my patience is slowly wearing thin—

But I'm not barefooting or fancy-free,
I don't take off in a moment's notice,
where the sunshine takes me.

Transparency
is a weird superpower
one wins to get
into the heart of things.

Emotional Holocaust

You now admire Kim Jong Un
after working with him,
after seeing how his powers of suggestion
dazzle his people—

The cult of personality passed down by his daddy
really affects the entire populace of his country,
and you want to attain a similar kind of undying power
while governing your followers
as you try to win the Nobel Peace Prize,
while sanctioning the many decades of tyranny
of North Korea's regime—

But what about the children?
The countless refugees and would-be immigrants to our
    country,
these innocents now brutally separated from their parents,
urgently trying to escape their home countries' regimes'
    rapes and murders
(a lot of North Koreans tried to escape to China after threats
    of death,
and why did they want to do that?)

Mr. President?
Are you going to say something about this?
Or…are you defending your new buddy
by covering your own ass?

All these young kids need *a shower*,
no goodbyes are necessary,
it's like leaving them at preschool,
all children cry—
It's no freaking preschool;
children are screaming bloody murder!
Are they losing their parents, possibly forever?

Hitler did this with the Jews,
separating parents from children
and husbands from wives,
all with the promise of a *shower* to clean up the mess

There were no more Hitlers in Germany or Austria after WWII;
that family name is now permanently erased.
Keep going along this path, Mr. President,
and there will be no more Trumps.
If your family members do have any hearts left,
they should distance themselves from your name
due to your sanctioned emotional holocaust—

Will your obsession with immortality
and sweet dreams of dictatorship
be worth all the pain you have caused?

(2/3rds of our country now view you as mad
since you hate the emotional power of whole, intact families
who are now uprooted violently by their tender hearts,

standing alone in stalemate
without a country,
their children taken away like pawns in a chess game?)

Is this worth it, this emotional holocaust that is creating
   your legacy
so you can be more like Kim Jong Un?

Crossing the Border

We are all trapped by the curve of our signatures.

Our histories are somewhat similar,
even though the names and locations we come from differ...
We are almost the same, but we are not the same.

We are carved in complementary shapes,
my skin on your skin, your skin on my skin, even when
reality blows forth an autumn chill, and we are nothing more
than friends,

Summer dreaming is as heavy as whipped cream;
our pseudo-children are golden and green,

but you don't feel the same, you don't share the same dream,
I let the sleeping kids lie.

I lie to myself, making lions out of tabbies, words are the only
currency I can afford,

music is the only God I pray to.

Could I will you to cross the border towards my side?
The girls are waiting to lie down,
sinking with the sun on the green.

Twenty Years

In twenty years
my sister might be put in the cold, cold ground
the worst possible case scenario
her body's slowly breaking down
(not just because of cancer)
her knees are shot
her stomach's rearing its ugly head with too much acid
constant indigestion, raspy cough
she can't bend her body at the waist
she lost all feeling in her arm

And her young kids
what will become of them?
Will they have to leave Texas
if the ultimate worst thing happens?

I dreamt once of her memorial service
my eyes are wetter than most rivers alive,
I'm hitting seventy
I see a sea of her friends in a full auditorium,
my eyes are underwater, swimming

Mom says:
I hope that I'm dead when that happens

My parents are strong as mighty oak trees
but a death of a child would split them open
no chance of survival, the wounds jagged
like a lightning bolt striking against perfect tree trunks,
capsizing

Twenty years may sound like forever
twenty years goes by in an eye-blink
leaving us all bewildered
in its passage of time

Will she be still alive then?

Suspended Animation

1.

Frozen—back in time
I should had been there the moment you fell

Now doctors have brought you back
since you were so
cold cold cold on the ground

You were trying to save someone's life
carving a new heart out of broken parts
you gave my life such a start
the very first moment I saw you

I saw you first please admit that
but will you ever say anything
out loud again

You look so sweet white on the sheet
the color's now back but barely
and you're asleep
the job's now done

Where are you now?
Why can't we reach you?
Why have I been such a chickenshit
for so many years?
Why can't you wake up?

You are warmed up—

2.

I'm not dead yet—
I've been watching you without me for a while
in an invisible room
in a nameless healing dimension

I was cold for a long time
I fell from the ledge as I was trying to save a life
maybe I was going to also save mine
since the cold had preserved my brain my heart and
    internal organs

Was I asleep for very long?
A part of me was watching everything
but I'm not dead—
they kept me frozen for a while
before they warmed me up

Did they carve out a new heart
and new working organs from the cold?
(Only you could ever believe that would be possible—
    I saw you
watching without me)

Both of us in suspended animation
until the same moment we do wake up
will we be no longer frozen?

Will we still care for each other?
I thought you were the one doing the leaving
but you're here
I'm still asleep
I need to regenerate
I need to sleep some more—

Army of Ghosts

Singing for her supper, this soothsayer
talked of war and love, and isolation,
she is haunted by actions past,
of past lovers and bad decisions,
back in blue with a vengeance

She has an army of ghosts
that protects her while she's sleeping.

Her whiskey-flavored words
can turn the hardest cynic around,
even when the army is fighting hard—

She charms the crowd like an old-time preacher
from the house of blues;
she loves all of us
more than we will ever know,
leaving all her sins in the dust
so the glitter could shine on.

Army Oranges

My head was swimming trying to follow bits of conversation
at the table and in the drawing room before lunch;
my husband plays the piano too loud,
my brother-in-law plays as well,
but too carefully, and the Crasta clan
has to leave early to attend a christening.

Later, after lunch, I asked Richard
if he was ever in the Navy.

Not exactly, he answered;
I was in the Yellow Berets,
the Medical Core while stationed
in Bethesda, so thank God
we weren't called into action
in 1975 (the end of Vietnam).

Then, Uncle Sam mentioned
navel oranges, if sailors only
get to eat them while at sea,
thereupon Richard added:

How about them Army Oranges?
They must fight hard!

Immediately after explaining the joke
(to no avail, no one was listening),
Uncle Sam and Richard debated about how to tell
a watermelon was ripe,
as a bowl of watermelon wedges
were being passed around
the table along with slithers of
Espagna sponge cake,
heavily scented
with orange peel.

It should sound hollow when you thump it!
No,
It should hear the seeds swimming inside; it should be solid!

The debate went on, as the ladies
rolled their eyes and ate homemade macaroons.

I was busy wondering
while sipping ice tea, if
Army Oranges did exist
at any time during any of the popular wars,
how they nourished the troops
as they fought on,
and perhaps they gave
some needed solace during the holidays.

I remember my grandfather's stories of WWII
in the Army Air Corps (before the Air Force),
as his squadron flew all around the world,
in a top-secret mission spying on airports.

Their oranges may have been
crafted to take flight,
as well as fight.

I miss Papa a little today,
but he wouldn't get the joke
about the oranges.

Remembrance Day

We should never forget
when we were the unwilling pawns of madmen

who ushered out death sentences
due to cults of personality,
who robbed good people blind for their own profits,
who tried to destroy historical objects and actual stories
    in order to get ahead,
who trapped those who were perceived as rats and pigs,
but were doves and gentle dogs trying to find their way home,
wandering in endless fields,
hidden in overgrown trees,
sailing in boats with no home port to escape to—

All the deaths, ongoing for many years,
the wasted hidden potentials snuffed out before their time,
possible cures and inventions to help humanity,
never realized,
families shattered, stripped, eschewed, abandoned, changed
    forever—

My husband's family,
half of its elder, original members that carried the torch
    for hundreds of years,
is now dust, thanks to war.

Genocide is still happening,
we haven't learned the lesson:
NO MORE
NO MORE

The slaughter continues;
will we ever learn to stop the senseless killing?
We must at least try to remember this,

no more killing,
please good people,
no more

Ursula (no. 58 of Women's Names Sensual Series)

Your mother named you
after the mighty spirit of a bear.
We barely saw you
before you able to stand—

Your mother is a strong woman,
they called her a witch,
your Dad is a true-blue
man of the Navy.

We wondered what happened to you,
dear girl; are you
a witch like your mother,
military like your father,
or are you your own person,
with your own life?

You should be 18 by now,
about to graduate.
Will you burst out the cave
of Choctaw, OK,
or will you dwell in
the dark forest forever?

I hope someday you
will be able to be seen,
safe from mediocrity,
not turned by tricksters
and charlatans,

able to roar deeply
using your own strong ideas
and inner beauty.

Frigg (no. 12 of Women's Names Sensual Series)

When I read about Wigga,
the Iron Age goddess-cook
in Gunter Grass's "The Flounder,"
my Viking side, receptor/protector
of 47% of my DNA
that until now, had lain dormant/silent
woke up.

She came in, in armor and dirt-covered clothes
ready, for either battle or planting,
like the ancient German Wigga
(who Grass created)

She stood strong, capable and determined,
reading my face as though it was a book and snorted
in derision; I wasn't woman enough for her yet.

I still loved her.
(She put the stony-faced New Englanders and pioneer
 women to shame…)

Holding a bulb of a future vegetable
in her beefy hands, she finally spoke:

You have waited here for a long time.
It is necessary; when one is ready
to work, to fight or to receive knowledge.

*One waits until he/she is ready,
and now, since you admire
my iron-clad, planter Goth sister
for her strength and fortitude,
how she bound the neighboring tribes together
by making the men toil the soil
so they didn't starve in dead winter.
Then some strong-willed
planters became fishers
and masters of the ocean,
sailed away in their mighty ships
to infiltrate far-away lands,
spilled their seed in red-haired women,
enjoyed their dominion and their
bloody claim to the lands of the Celts
as conquerors of the misty moors…but
though we women may have remained behind,
my curious girl,
the land remained our prize, our birthright.
We are the creators of life, fire and food,
we keep all who dwell here alive.
I see that you keep morale alive
thanks to your voice and words
that you invent on empty pages.
Don't ever lose that.*

*Understand if I ever stopped
to cry about our situation,*

as others tend to do,
I might as well have lain down dead,
because we all
will be dead
if women give into sadness…

I lost family, babies and men,
but I keep moving to survive…

So, keep moving!
Winter will come. Get ready for it.

Then she moved on;
there she was a spot away
planting bulbs in the earth
with her bare hands,
clawing the ground open.

Elegy for Hawking

Was Stephen Hawking a poet?
Yes, he wrote of the cosmos as if it was a beloved, mysterious
    lover.

Black holes, quantum mechanics, a brief history of Time,
he was known for these things, not just for his ailments,
his brain was a complete wondrous thing, to be brilliant
in the most progressive and transgressive of times.

Poetic that he died on Pi Day,
the most mystical of all-known numbers, constantly evolving
    & growing,
drifting into space, forever changing & computing—
perhaps we will eventually find a bit of Hawking's essence
floating forever in the stars, constantly computing &
    evolving,
never standing still—

Mind-Thought Police
(based on Radiohead's "Karmic Police")

Mind-thought police,
arrest that man
staring too much at that side-boob;
go catalog his porn star fantasy
backlogs
where girls don't mind a grabbed snatch—

Mind-thought police,
arrest that lady
she's waiting to implode,
this world has no soul left,
she joins a weird cult and now carries a gun—

Instantly there's karma you all must deal with,
if you do it wrong, you'll mess it up,
the butterfly's already flapped its wings
and caused an explosion

Mind-thought police,
please subdue my nephew's ADD tendencies
to go to the mat slamming his sister
whenever he acts up

Mind-thought police,
please place a weapon in my niece's hands,
if she's thrown to the mat by her brother,
or anyone else,
she has to learn to defend herself

Is this was you wanted,
a kingdom built of chaos?
All the good knights have left
to take a smoke break,
sharpening their weapons.

Mind-thought police,
move these cars faster across the bridge,
this baby's gotta keep warm
and earn her living for another day more

For a while, I've lost myself
but now I'm waking up
but the snooze dial's still humming loudly—

Tainted (Until Now)
(no. 37 of E verses)

Our water's been tainted;
our children no longer can walk up straight,
the iron had clotted their blood supply,
robbing them of needed minerals.

Our words have been tainted;
more idiots have been elected,
and real news is wearing thin,
polluting all of our minds into pulp.

Our own judgements have been tainted until now;
women were afraid to speak up
when men touched them in places they shouldn't,
fearing certain recourse, they've shut up, until now;

Men could get away with anything at all,
but young boys and men are now learning
that young girls and women are human beings,
not carved out of sex and whipped cream,
scheming their downfall for a potent kiss.

Have the teaching of our forefathers
have grown tainted over the years?

Until now, we can avoid most poisons,
our physical, verbal, and psychological-made ones
by finding out the naked truth for ourselves.

Dark Thoughts

1.

I was taught to stand only in the light;
dark thoughts were works of the Devil
and must be avoided at all costs.

Among these dark thoughts,
I want to kiss my husband passionately
in public, along with someone else,
without embarrassment (from him)
or judgement (to me),
since I never did sign up
for one lover, forever
like he did…

And, among the darkest tendrils,
was wishing for suicide at a tender age,
destructive tendencies in mid-teens,
and wishing I was anywhere else--

Even now, in New York City,
the rest of the world still tempts me;
even now, in this long-term relationship,
I want to kiss someone else;
even now, standing in a safe place,
I want to stand in a rocky place
and the watch the swirling waters turn
from my window

2.

My sister from marriage
paints her face in harsh black and purple,
her goth-nature welcomes the dark side
as a devoted mistress.

Sometimes she puts on her game face
in front of her newborn son,
who wears a face of sunshine.

*He has to learn that his Mama
looks like this sometimes,*
as she paints her claws
fresh for evening.

She's the coolest mother ever,
he will be ready for the world
and its complexities…

3.

My Mama hid all the dark impulses,
she only believed in the Light:

Sex is hidden deep in a brown wrapper,
hardly opened or discussed—
my dark wants are still spanking new
(ooh, there's a new one there I want to try),
but why didn't Mama teach me about this?

4.

Ignoring it doesn't make it go away;
nighttime comes naturally, but then in the worst way,
people bow towards violence (hiding abuse)
and ignorance (she never said anything was wrong),
and a lot of dark thoughts are perverted and twisted
according to society at large.

We should be aware of both sides,
and dwell in both of them, until the place
we eventually find is lit perfectly,
holding many shades of possibilities.

Dark Matter (In Human Scale)

It may not be just theoretical,
heavy dark matter-crushing particles, that leave
behind no footprint or radiation, once disguised
as ancient stars that died out long ago,
now they can take down future starships.

People can carry the dark matter
in their psyches for years, the sickness
clouds the bloodstream, becomes the
welcoming ghost in their bed,
crushing them, while still alive,
as they wait for new stars to germinate,
to warm their bones once again

To fight the matter, one must
smile in one's liver, then in every cell
until the darkness stops.

River Styx Today (No. 36 Of E Verses)

Don't worry lady,
you only visited the first two Underworlds
thanks to the fire.

The first passage was encased in smoke pillars;
you had to hold your breath in
so you could grab the key
hiding under the water.

(The River Styx is too crowded with hopeful individuals
who wanted a bit of Heaven, but they missed their chance
to negotiate with favors & trinkets to the guys Upstairs
about the overall value of their lives before this)

Only Persephone made it through all nine levels.
She fell hard for the head honcho when
she was still young & green;
a real momma's girl, she was…
Now she spends half of the year in New York.

&, thanks to a similar understanding,
the key to the lock fits, & you had opened
the door to the second level.
How was your experience?

We thought for a minute you had died,
but you gasped out water out of your lungs
as your body happily swayed upon the grass.

Dance with Death
(Remembering Nana, 1925-2006)

Her dance with death
began when her man,
she'd married to for almost 60 years
died from an aggressive, sudden cancer

For two years
she prayed for God to take her,
refusing any extra food,
she always slept,
only rising for her daily coffee and multiple cigarettes.

She was a great dancer;
entertaining for the boys in the USO
during WWII,
participating in neighborhood Follies
with her man and friends,
teaching her children and grandchildren effective steps
to charm and attract others' attention

At the end
she remained frozen in place,
waiting for her fatal dance with Death
until he finally took her out—

so she could be with
her man again,
she waited so long
to take her final steps.

Haunted

Bones of forgotten angels in water, floating
on the screen as "Pyramid Song"
played in my ears for the first time,
as I tried the imagine the night
that Charles Mingus crafted his catchy tune,
performed it as his "Freedom",
that it sparked many good things forward,
like for Thom Yorke and his crew—

I am bounded by trash,
memories are trapped within objects
I can't throw away yet, lest I'll forget them;
my clothes gathering on the chest-of-drawers,
ransacked, in various degrees of cleaning-ness
only I can decipher. My a-la-modes sense of decodes
are slowly gathering dust, the lust of new items
pale after the initial claim, a bargain becomes a tempest
residing on the other side of the wall, waiting to be
dug up again, in a year or so, when someone else
(who knows who?) complained about the smell.

I'm haunted by bad decisions, my man
needs to rekindle his childhood daily
after many stressful weeks, weakened
by his own sicknesses, he won't let go,

he won't let them go, the monsters and bullies
that had infected his brain, an humming virus
making him alone, almost like a robot sometimes.

I saw his blue eyes and I fell deep, too fast,
never knowing about the emotional crap
we would both mine out together,
and the objects that would remain out of reach.

In Passing (No. 45 Of E Verses)

Maybe none of us truly *arrive*—
Even at the point of death
each sweet soul is still searching

for closure, peace, and meaning.
Each one of us is the same person
one is born as: the kindnesses witnessed,
the failings felt, the sins committed,
the lessons repeated until mastery---

until passing into the Great Beyond,
into the rest of the grand Universe,
we fold with constellations of stars
until we become stars,

but our souls, our inner selves
remain the same forever,
no matter where we eventually end up.

Angels on the Shelf (No. 43 Of E Verses)

Faces of numerous angels stare blankly on,
perched upon the living room mantle at Nana's house,
keeping her company for many years.

Her new dog is here after Papa died,
and her cigarettes, and Mom and Dad,
but her angels are her babies.

Most of them were bought for having faces
resembling her grandchildren;
it was creepy seeing my angel-self
staring back at my real-self
from the shelf—

Where did all the angels disappear to after she died?
Did they resurface on the tabletops of cousins,
or did they reemerge in human form,
giving backrubs to playboy grandpas on the bus?

I don't need a frozen angel;
I have the Universe.

White is the Color of Death

An apartment of 20 years
suddenly becomes empty,
leaving only the glass table
and the white walls behind.

I showed up at the end of the
Universe, armed with coffee
and money tips for the moving men,
but before we all departed,
the books I carried to the basement
were bound up by the super
in white-clear garbage bags;
I felt my heart breaking instantly...

There are three things one
should never see made into ash:
People, pets and books.

Before dinner, we saw both
the gleaming Empire State Building
and the One Freedom Tower,
both lit up by white lights.

White is the color of death,
he said while crossing Bleecker Street.

The dead one was a past crush of this,
unconsummated;
he wasn't the desired one back then,
but now, everyone knows and wants him.
But his friend is now suddenly gone;
he was a year older than him.

And I am strangely happy at the end
even in muted sadness during a rushed dinner;
he played for our supper.
The Haydn nocturne in E-flat major
was beautiful and soothing.

Will our sadness fade into white?
I had to leave at 9:30.
Funny, I thought all white cats loved long, black coats.

Born in Norman, Oklahoma, Carrie Magness Radna is an archival audiovisual cataloger at the New York Public Library, a singer, a lyricist-songwriter, and a poet who loves to travel. Her poems have previously appeared in the *Oracular Tree, Tuck Magazine, Muddy River Poetry Review, First Literary Review-East, Mediterranean Poetry, Shot Glass Journal, The Poetic Bond VIII*, and *The spirit, it travels: an anthology of transcendent poetry* (Cosmographia: published August 3, 2019) and will be published in *Nomad's Choir, Polarity e-Magazine* and *The Poetic Bond IX*. Her first chapbook, *Conversations with Dead Composers at Carnegie Hall* (Flutter Press) was published on January 18, 2019, and *Remembering You As I Go Walking* (Boxwood Star Press) was published on

August 23, 2019. She won third prize for "The Tunnel" (Category: Words on the Wall: All-Genre Prompt) at the 69th annual Philadelphia Writers' Conference (2017). She also won 12th place "Lily (no. 48 of Women's names sensual series)" by the 2018 *Writer's Digest* Poetry Awards. She is a member of the Greater New York Music Library Association (GNYMLA), and is a member of the New York Poetry Forum, Parkside Poets, Riverside Poets, Brownstone Poets and Nomad's Choir. When she's not performing classical choral works with Riverside Choral Society or New Year's Eve performances with the New York Festival Singers, or writing art song lyrics with her choir buddies, or traveling, she lives with her husband Rudolf in Manhattan.

www.ingramcontent.com/pod-product-compliance
Lightning Source LLC
Chambersburg PA
CBHW030132100526
44591CB00009B/621